OF ANNUNCIATIONS

OF ANNUNCIATIONS

EWA CHRUSCIEL

OMNIDAWN PUBLISHING
OAKLAND, CALIFORNIA
2017

Cover painting by Julie Püttgen:
Cloudmapping: Next Gate, 2008.
Watercolor and gouache on paper, 16 x 12 inches
www.108namesofnow.com & www.unlessanduntil.info.

Cover typeface: Trajan Pro & Garamond 3 LT Std.
Interior typefaces: Garamond 3 LT Std, Trajan Pro,
& Palatino LT Std.

Cover & Interior design by Cassandra Smith

Offset printed in the United States
by Edwards Brothers Malloy, Ann Arbor, Michigan
On 55# Enviro Natural 100% Recycled 100% PCW
Acid Free Archival Quality FSC Certified Paper

Library of Congress Cataloging-in-Publication Data

Names: Chrusciel, Ewa, author.
Title: Of annunciations / Ewa Chrusciel.
Description: Oakland, California : Omnidawn Publishing,
    2017. | Includes bibliographical references.
Identifiers: LCCN 2017020702 | ISBN 9781632430397
    (paperback : alk. paper)
Classification: LCC PS3603.H78 A6 2017 | DDC 811/.6--dc23
LC record available at https://lccn.loc.gov/2017020702

Published by Omnidawn Publishing, Oakland, California
www.omnidawn.com   (510) 237-5472   (800) 792-4957
        10 9 8 7 6 5 4 3 2 1
        ISBN: 978-1-63243-039-7

TABLE OF CONTENTS

You do not count for anyone, you should be grateful for being tolerated among us. Civilized people need not be gentle with foreigners. "That's it, and if you don't like it why don't you go back where you came from!" The humiliation that disparages the foreigner endows his master with who knows what petty grandeur.

Julia Kristeva, *Strangers to Ourselves*

The arrival of the refugees dismantles our normalized social dysfunction on more than one level. It recalls another world, perhaps a real one, outside of the bubble filled with complacency and anxiety in equal measure, as we keep imitating the lifestyles of the rich and going into debt in order to fashion and maintain our pathetic simulacra.

Izabela Morska, *Glorious Outlaws: Debt as a Tool in Contemporary Postcolonial Fiction*

The poet's limbs lay scattered
Where they were flung in cruelty or madness,
But Hebrus River took the head and lyre
And as they floated down the gentle current
The lyre made mournful sounds

Ovid, *Metamorphoses*

NON-MIGRANTS' QUESTIONS

What can you do, migrants? Calcified birds.
You perch on the trees at night.
You wear painted masks of scarabs. You have beaks.
You cast your nests. You pine on trees.
You needle. You roam the woods.
You wade through the freeze.
You come in a veil. You wait under a black chador.
You churn up grains, tides, whispers—
Your feet, dark banished nests, stitched wings of—
You perch in a fog. You sit on the camphor tree.
On a branch, on invisible stretchers. On a log, you pound.
It is a drumming station. On a log you pound your wings
until the dogwood hears.
You jump out of mouths with clumps of green.
With forsythia. You jump out of doorknobs.
You feather the chairs. Swallows exclaim the air.
Your feet—a precipice. Throat tips, ink stained. Miraculous
displacement—
Whisper the cliffs. Pound wings until the whole forest hears
until the logs spark into lumens.

MIGRANTS' ANNUNCIATION

Stones in our mouths,
barefoot we climb
rocks. We walk on eggs;
we tap the earth.

Each foot chants dust
we swallow. Our mouth, granular,
sealed. Our feet rock away
from crucifixions.

These rocks were feathers first—
magma and birds into earth,
charcoal lines, into waiting

shifting, memory
flicks red. Pilgrims, we
follow a spirit
of mountain up to a cross.

Blood trickles out of our mouths.
We stare into the lines of sacrifice.

The boat sways,
we comb our hair.

§

Trees branch under water
breathe, triangulate, bivalve.

The roots spawn our universe,
the size of a grapefruit.

A tiger, in a shock of vision,
tamed into a clock.

Each clock has an Archangel
who carves into an aspen

a bark cradle
for each world.

There are spoils:
herons and storks,
silver foxes basking in cemeteries.

Each world has saints and dybbuks
& three other dimensions:

oils and wicks,
cherries and figs
of dark.
St. George & a dragon;
its teeth tick,
each tick spawns a migrant.

§

Out of Archangel's lungs
an air plant,
a cringe—from this a yes.
Morphemes, consonants,
suspension bridges, sea-horses,
mint, Nantucket knots—
in yes the sea nests
prayer and curse
to bless, to wound.

§

The air wrinkles
a stone.
Water into sticks
& dust,

into trenches, corals,
hieroglyphs. Locks
onto a page, miniscule—

a migrant, hyperbole,
juxtaposition of incompatibles,
from a place that is not our own.

I See Men, But They Look Like Trees, Walking

Spruce & pine, fir & birch,
hornbeam & beech washed ashore.
These trees were migrants first.

Wrath, sea urchins and anemones, ferns.
Hedgehogs of dried flowers and thorn crowns.

The branches conceal seeds
without shore or limit

walking trees,
in fishing boats, on rafts.
Dust blows
bodies onto the shore,

gingkoes, excavators,
makers of eyes.

The trees are brides and frogs and green crumbs,
storing air.

These trees under water breathe.
The refugees rain inside their breathing.

§

Dybbuk grows inside the tree,
an air plant, an epiphyte,
a figure of speech, a departure.

§

Out of Archangel's lungs
a cloud spawned yes, a nebula.
A contraction, really.
It takes a million particles for the core to ignite.
The foxes hurtle and flame.

Out of the swan's bone, a flute, out of the griffin's bone,
a flute, out of the cave bear's femur, a flute, the oldest,
out of the mammoth's tusk, a flute, out of the wing bones of red-
crowned cranes, a flute, out of the vulture's bone,
a flute. The air lives in holes. Out of a solid apparition, silence.
Out of nebula, a whale. Apparitions web the sea.

§

Within each migrant, a canticle. Silence of a flute.
Now, each fold, a loss, absent a miracle unless a finch
in the air, a paper into a beast. Each crease an angle,
a power line draws an ineluctable arrow. A migrant
on a wire, a balancing warbler – still, motionless, forward.
A foot here, a hand there: zero, plus ultra, non.
Ropes and knots. Words, which secure the body.
Which the soul? When the rock falls, when lips in the dark;
confusion is sacred. Catchword to break the sound.

WE ARE THE BRIDE

We were stuck for two days amidst the bombs in Ashrafiya.

A 10-year-old boy came in with a knife carrying

a wedding dress.

He cut the dress into many pieces and gave us each a piece.

We wore it on our heads and went out into the streets.

When snipers see it, they stop shooting.

What if we crossed Europe in wedding dresses,

our wavelengths stretching infinitely.

Migrant Woman Dreams of Love

Sing me away:

on these jagged shores

my cheekbones

pomegranates.

I cannot count the kisses.

Let me repose with my love in an apricot tree.

REFUGEE'S DAILY PRAYER

The house cracked from the inside.
It plaited and meandered in waves.
The tree and the house grew into one.

The bark entered the house,
inmates of shrines of cicadas.

A medieval tower with a clock
blasted vertically,
with no slant
on its knees,
and the clock
swooped like an owl,
grabbed all the hours &
disappeared.

Change the stone to bread.

Give back the salt
and let olives be relics.

Volunteer's Premonitions

Then, what are blackberries
if not our longing for pine needles & whirs,
the sea inside them
transfigured?

What are the ferns, particles, and saints?
Trees underwater breathe circumferences,
hourglasses, cliffs
into radiance.

What is the loon that descends
us into silences?

What are these empty spaces
between the households?

ARCHANGEL APPEARS TO A MIGRANT

"Leave towards endlessly stretching waves."

There is no lily, I say.
His voice rushed:
"Take your child; take your SIM card, and your rosary
beads, photos and a radio, one plush toy."

"How could it be?" I thought, but all I let out of me
was: "Yes, be it done."

I wanted His fluttering wings to carry me,
but they flew on to the next household, bullets
in His feathers. The annunciation did not recur,
so I confused a smuggler for an Archangel.
The boat was inflatable, unstable.
Now, the processions of faces in the waves, staring
into the house I knew nothing about.
The sea was bound to shake.

A SETTLER SPEAKING FROM THE SHORE

The sea keeps its apparitions, spits out
migrants, walking trees. Branches
conceal seeds without shore or limit.
In blue-bin bags they carry what
they have, beg for change,
cell phones, sleeping bags.
Some money blows over barbed wire.
Swaddled in Armani, Gucci, Dior, they get
on boats. Dust blows pairs of sneakers, torn up
tents, toothbrushes, bodiless acts
of exiles, a Syrian toddler. Synapses and quarks
fleck the sky. The grass, the air, the phlox, each
count the routes of their return. They lift two thousands
bee balms and foxgloves to the light. Splashers of transparency,
pollinators of the ineffable,
check the pulse of air.

LULLABY FOR THE STILL OBJECTS

Fashion, a tale of *walfisch*; wolves turned into water-kites. Astral
liquids in measured strains. Confident

chiasmus in dream—
stations
which is to say, let it be stone

that propels its foliage to the Sea. Shoots
and thistles, wild grapes wild grapes and gooseberries
take hedge

give grazing thorns and briers.

Cloud which puts forth its foliage to the Sea
and turns into a bone –

it will be a cornerstone
as far as the river,

which is to say *wieloryb* or *balena*

of radiance – ika moana. A rather
spherical being;
duende and knots.

You know each
to its own peacocky rain and bow.

§

Inside the sea the river
rivulets. Inside the sea three thousand
carry valises, Simcards, photos, coats,
multiple editions of the Koran and Bible,
faces of children.

Dybbuk painted himself with waves
to steal their three thousand bundles.

Inside the river, death cradles,
stretches, triangulates.

OF ANNUNCIATIONS

Now the painting is haunted
by *pentimenti*,
incisions,
ghost rays.
True annunciation happens
in the dark lines of wood grain,
in red wax seals, in three tapered wood dowels,
a bonsai tree —
so small, it could fit
into a crack in the sidewalk.

A Homeless EU Migrant Woman

There are feathery witnesses
in a great cloud on every side of us.
The river seeps through a man's hands.
The streets, in canvases, seep through cracks,
hisses, chutes, pitches, shrieks.
An alien sits on the curb.
Children carry albatrosses into a cathedral –
the souls of the righteous are infants
banksias, matted sedge,
hanging swamps.

Carousels whirling inside the river.
Wooden horses, gypsies,
the river seeps through feathers.
An old woman in skirt of many skirts,
whirling in her mouth the cubes of sugar
(stolen from a bookstore).
The carousel goes round and round.
Queen of the Arno, wooden horses,
Gypsies, circumferences –
until the woman kneels
from too many cubes, carouselin
from her mouth.

What praise –
the light of last seen wounds.
Heron riffles its diagonal tail,
a cross, a comma amidst tectonic plates.

The river eddies, backflows,
crests into her temples.

Until she kneels before the Duomo
and vomits back its oozing sweetness
she could not use.

The Fox Lingers

A comet flames through the sea.

Air hurries onward.

The fox, a polycandela,
lights the forest.

How many arguments of asteroids does it take? The light,
a donor. Epiphyte intends to grow in a dark cloud.

Migrants stare into the house they know nothing about.

MIGRANTS DREAM UNDER WATER

We are an emergency room.
Will litanies arrive?

We are the house and the tree,
in somebody else's story.

We pass the field of poppies;
we collect red graffiti,

sacred nouns,
red relics.

Psalms spread their tents
and light their cigarettes.

Who gathers the waters of the sea into jars?

The sea maims its apparitions—
pots, books, locks, chargers,
boots, shoes, sandals, cassette
tapes, fillers, openers, multiple
editions of the Koran, glasses, pictures
of saints, rosaries, photos, sweatpants,
balls, toys, bags, plates, bottles, wrenches,
relics, footnotes, unidentified sounds,
pieces of wedding dresses, enjambed
passages.

The number of objects exceeds endings.
The wavelengths stretch
metonymies of perpetual
orders, empty from
possessions, haunted
by *pentimenti*.

Will you carry these things just as *San Miniato*
carried his head across the river?

Volunteer Dreams

An oak branches under the water,
bifurcates, and & and & and, (litany
of ampersands), whales and waltzes.

I write these letters carefully not to mangle our alphabet.
Will you arrive like a sparrow, finding God's small things in the
quotidian cracks?
Will you arrive like a tigress, hungry and slinking.

As a lotus lives in its water, I, rooted in you.

§

Icicles and cataracts, hour-glasses and thorns.
Each immigrant, a footnote.

Weeds in barren ground.

We do not own our cites.
We do not own our bodies.

Dybbuk grows inside the sea,
an air plant, an epiphyte.

Be Still, the Lord Is
On Your Side

They arrive with laments and prayers,
in life jackets of sinking couch foam –
$25 each on top of thousands of dollars
paid to the smugglers to get on the dinghies.
We flicker the lights on the beach in Lesbos.
The flow of peripheries until the center emerges.
They paddle on their dinghies, coterminous route
to the ferry: Ayvalık, Turkey – Mytilini, Lesvos
for only 15 Euros.

If they see us and stand up out of desperation or excitement, they
will tip the dinghy over.

Exilium

I lost my husband. I could not find him during the firing in
Hama. I took my ID with me, and my four children. My mother
and my 13 siblings live in Turkey. I am told life is easier there.
One day I hope to join them. My name is Hayam. I am 37.

The most important thing I took from Syria is my SIM card for
my old phone, which is inactive now, but I keep the SIM card.
When I reached Lebanon, all I had with me was a plastic bag. My
name is Ahmad. I am 25.

I took fear with me. When it strikes, I take my children and
run. When we ran the first time, we took a plastic bag with
documents and photographs. My daughter took her Tweety Bird.
She keeps her eye on it and in the evening she puts all the candies
she has inside it. My name is Muhammad. I am 38.

I took photos of my family and friends when I left our house in
Tel Kelekh during the gunfire. Bullets perforated the walls. After
crossing the border with Lebanon, I saw on YouTube that our
house was demolished. My name is Joanna. I am 22.

I brought with me a wooden box which I bought in Baba Sharqi,
a district of Damascus. The box is decorated with mussel shells. I
keep my guitar picks in it. My name is Adnan. I am 25.

I took with me my fiancé's lighter. It is an ordinary lighter. He
wanted it back, but I never gave it to him. I did not tell my fiancé
I was leaving. He supported Assad. I supported the revolution.
We did not talk about politics, to avoid conflict. My name is
Noor. I am 21.

I keep prayer beads, called *tasbih*, which means "to travel swiftly."
I had them on my neck when we left the house in Al-Raqqah. I
take them off when I shower. There are 99 beads for 99 names for
Allah. My name is Halima. I am 45.

I took golden bracelets from our house in Aleppo with me. I sold
them to buy a tent in Lebanon. My name is Mariam. I am 23.

We took a kerosene lamp. We knew there were power outages in
Lebanon every four hours. My mother, Fawza, took her sewing
machine, which she's had since childhood. We also took an old
mortar. [the name missing]

I took a key with me. I come from Tel Kelekh in Homs province.
Fayez, 25 years old.

Even though we left in the summer, I took a red winter jacket, a
present from my father. Ruba, 4 years old.

I could not take my pigeons from Daara. My brother told me
how to raise them and train them. I fed them out of my hands.
Hussein, 16 years old.

I took my radio with me. I don't let anybody touch it. When I
leave the room, I close it in my wardrobe. I know the frequency
& exact time of broadcasts. It is like being lost in the sea. The
waves take you in all directions. I know the sea. I live in it. Ali,
70 years old.

I took a scar on my belly. Ahmad, 65 years old.

I took a photo of my cousin, who drowned in the river while
crossing the border with Lebanon. Khalil, 24 years old.

I took a cloth, *tantal* in Kurdish. My sister made it. The light beams out of it. Juma, 33 years old.

I took the Koran with me. I keep it in a special suitcase. Haj Zaher, 51 years old.

I took a photo of my lost son. He was 16 when they arrested him. I have not seen him since. Ibtissam, 40 years old.

§

Do not regret a crocus when woods are on fire

GUARDIAN ANGEL OF EXODUS

Do not mistreat or oppress a foreigner, for you were foreigners in Egypt.

You must not mistreat or oppress foreigners in any way. Remember, you yourselves were once foreigners in the land of Egypt.

You shall not wrong a sojourner or oppress him, for you were sojourners in the land you knew nothing about.

You shall not wrong a stranger or oppress him, for you were strangers in the land of your refuge.

Thou shalt neither vex a stranger, nor oppress him: for ye were strangers in the land of the strange, home of others not you.

You must not exploit a foreign resident or oppress him, since you were foreigners in the land of your forsaken hope.

You are not to wrong or oppress an alien, because you were aliens in the land of new opening.

You must not wrong a foreigner nor oppress him, for you were foreigners in the land of a sudden horizon.

Never mistreat or oppress foreigners, because you were foreigners living in a sudden despair, suddenly disowned.

And a stranger shalt thou not wrong, neither shalt thou oppress him; for ye were strangers in the land of your oppressors.

Thou shalt neither mistreat a stranger nor oppress him; for ye were strangers in the land of your changed life.

You shall not wrong an alien, neither shall you oppress him, for you were aliens in the land of what you know not how to become.

VOLUNTEER – DREAMS

Making love with the Dark One and eating little,
those are my pearls and my carnelians.

In the sea—the figures stretch infinitely—

The monotony of bells, wound-
spread lilies.

We wake to the sound of trees, silver foxes
basking in the cemeteries.
Branches chatter into bells, icicle birds—
their wings, what wings?

Frostbitten, icicled wings,
octagonal owls,
what cathedrals are we to build?

Baptistery of octopi, windows flap
with holy hissing orchids.
St. George bludgeons the dragon
who floods the air.
The river seeps through a man's hands,
seeps through cracks, hisses chutes,
pitches.

A refugee sits on the curb and listens
to students reading love poems.

We want to wake into bells.
Cradled into hollows,
we carve nautilus patterns onto the stiff sea.

We drill holes in the ice. We make bonfires
with words, light up cemeteries.

VOLUNTEER – ROUGH NOTES

I am on the beach with seventy
irate young men. I keep calling Doctors
Without Borders. The doctors warn me against scabies.
Men stand in a ring. They set their blankets on fire.
I walk around hugging them. Will you marry me –
one after another says. I implore them not to burn the beach.

A ten-year-old boy approaches me:
Smoke?! Smoke! He repeats.
The confusion is infinite.
Finally I get it and we share a cigarette.

Volunteer – Rough Notes 2

In the camp, we distribute clothes. They need shoes
desperately. But people often send spangled slingback
shoes, unwashed evening gowns & prom dresses,
wedding garters, tents full of holes.

SETTLER FROM THE SHORE

The Sea suspends its apparitions.
The refugees rain inside
the trees under the sea.
The branches conceal the seeds
into mulberries,
into bodiless acts.

The sea develops a film.
Or what I meant to say:
refugees are the film on the ocean
inside its dark, nutrient
chambers.

Migrant Woman Dreams of Her Lover

What air delineates
seas.

Enjambed
passages.

Ether spits out blown,
finally projecting forward.

To grow oaks,
to roast acorns.
A raw seed
that smolders—

To grow oaks,
while you carry
lakes over your head.
These barks grow boats
of hourglasses under the water,
branching crowns.

Mountains hold water within them.

A Volunteer's Annunciation

A mountain has spilled out of her hands.
She bent to pick it up; there was an air wave,
undulation—bones to bones to a new mound.
A migrant dwells in the air where the mountain was.
Every circle, the dawn breaks.

There is a torn photograph where the mountain was.
Geologists gather to trace the cracks.
She bends to eat mica out of the blades;
by now all the balconies she constructed
over the precipice
faded away.

THE MIGRANT DREAMS OF WATER

Who Has Wrapped Up
the Waters in a Cloak?

In the pulsating voyage,
where does the water migrate?
Stars are fasting.
Water has a mouth.
Down in its dark rooms,
the ocean develops
me from its negative
until I grow insensitive
to light,

until I shed roots.

Cuvier's beaked whale dwells
deep down; ascends only
for a crack
of light

and then dives back.

THE GUARDIAN ANGEL OF THE WAVES

Water is indelible with apparitions. Current suspends
in the air.
It flickers; it bivalves. The fox lingers.

The bread has nerves, whispers,
comes from light
calcified into a vase.

Bread gone wild, an earthly planet,
a Cuvier's beaked whale.

TELEGRAM

     e   i

We f l   wat a t d bo f   th
min

We flo in   wate am th de bod fo   thir

We f loat in   water   amo the dea bodi for thirt
minu

we f l o a t w i w n a t a m e r o n g t h e a d b o d i e s f o r
d e t h i r t y

We float in water among the dead bodies for
thirty minutes.

A Prayer of a Non-Migrant

We stand on the beach in Lesbos and flash the lights
for the dinghies, in the night.

We carry the lights over
to bounce the darkness, just like the pilgrims'
paper lanterns scatter the dark for the Divine.

A woman throws her infant to me. It is icy cold.
Afraid to reanimate it, I start crying
for help, but the beach is empty.

Each grain stretches
in wavelengths.
Each grain grows
into a precipice.

I keep holding her hand
but it does not hold up
to the landscape, its throbbing.

To stay and to stand,
to be steadfast.

My hand empty
of possession.

The vespers I sang
in the void
fade away.

The infant girl whimpers, her breath shallow.
Was it the warmth of my body?

Refugee's Poem

How long shall we float,
almost *near a gleaming source of life –*
each wave, a face, a wake?
Had we perhaps entered the heart from the mouths
of guns? The waves tightened over us.
A wave spawns a face; a face spawns another face.
"Here you are," whisper the seaweed.
You confused archangels with smugglers.
You confused psalm for hourglass.
Holy Trinities on trees remain silent.
"Give us back our identity," we implore the waters.
"Trapped," hums the voice in a wave, "trapped by dust."
As if another God, will the God of Coast Guards
take care of us? Only the violent can carry away
the violence. "How long shall we float on our dinghies,
oh Lord? When we floated in water, the Red Cross did not help
us. The helicopters flew over us – took some photos for the news
and took off."
We have waited a long time, oh God
until when
oh God
tell us
until when

Poem of Memorial Day Weekend

Three days with three sunken ships
on the Mediterranean Sea,

seven hundred drowned in terms of the generalizations.

These vessels the sea finds unworthy.

These refugees the sea finds worthy.

Some float with necklace crosses in their mouths.

Heaves of storm
failed us.

Windows had wrung the light.
A thousand keepsakes
gather the moment of

Refugee Reminisces Capsizing

There were pigmy sea horses there. The waves kept stitching.
How to translate the colors? Figure is always
a departure. Words, lights peculiar to thoughts.
We stitched miraclets. On the other side of the moon,
on the reverse. To stay and to stand, to share all the words of
the pines and birches, *hyperbaton*. How can the prayers hold up a
landscape? The moon around the quilt
was nothing but dust reflecting nothing
but a speck of light, a holy
direction.

LEFT-TO-DIE BOAT

The helicopter hovered above our boat, dropped eight bottles of water, biscuits, cubes of sugar and left. The fishermen dried out their nets, almost capsizing our vessel. And left. The coastguard left. We drank water and urine. Where were our Guardian Angels? The oceanographers saw us. Trapped in waves, we yearn to exist. The water, left to witness. Let sorrowful longing dwell in our sugar-cube spit, lost in the waves. Shall we arrive as grebes or pelicans?

§

Language is a tern that transposes the borders. Do souls have a
language? Souls recede into words; *ab ovo*. How do they hatch
from boats—leaking ribcages, a shelter? A caesura in the sea.
Sometimes the moon throws a shadow of the cradle. The soul
carries annunciations, opening its
dazzling hands.

LOST AT SEA, COLD AND PLANETARY, THEY LONG FOR NARRATIVE

This is what the dead seek, to hurry back to bodies, to steep in
souls and grow large with each new one. *Metanoia*—
a word to grow fat on. Will an existing soul and a drowned one
unite, work side-by-side taking turns? Disembodiment hurts.
Each soul desires address. Hunting for home, a dark business. For
now they wade through the waves, they refract flashlights and
they bend on the surface of water, or, they roam on the beach,
tapping sand. They perch in a fog; they churn up grains, tides,
whispers. Will it be a jar that catches me like the wind?

VOLUNTEER'S NOTES

They are soaked, cold.

We lay them one by one on cardboard boxes.

Two Afghan brothers, aged three and seven, resuscitated next to each other.

One survives.

To rub the ice-cold hands of a child.

To give oxygen to a toddler.

Behind, the wailing of the mother.

When the white van drove into the graveyard
with bodies inside, the female volunteers were asked
to carry the corpses of women and children.

§

They pay $13,000 to die.
Some, afraid they'll die, put a necklace cross in their mouth.

The day before the shipwreck, she was singing Palestinian
songs:
"Lina Builds Her Tomorrows."

§

Pray to the crosses in their mouths.

GUARDIAN ANGEL OF OFFERING

We want God. Instead we have the poor, gang rapes, prostitution in the camps. You have been told that most of them are young, strong, single men. Ten thousand unaccompanied children had gone missing within Europe in 2016. The Pope says: "Migrants are not a danger—they are in danger." You have been told these men cut or burn the skin of their fingers not to be traced. There are children, too, without hands to beg or pray. They are the invisible in these lines. They sit on an invisible stretcher and beat with their wings. They whimper. We want to adopt them, but they are uncatchable. Only the dybbuks remain. They borrow us as vessels to get to the shore. We have the poor with us, but we climb over them through the abstractions to our gods.

§

And now the eternal, cramped
into cutting vegetables,
watering the meals.
Banana banana sep sep
halas, which means:
one banana per child.
But they keep coming back
for another – for their sister, brother,
mother, grandmother
(who are always sleeping).

We keep saying to them *halas* – done, finished.
The kids give us a nickname:
Banana banana sep sep
halas

§

Five-year-old Syrian boy

in a red t-shirt
washed ashore at Turkish Bodrun,
his tiny white sneakers
bobbing up.

The waves contract them in in
out out.

His entry shimmers,
his mouth full of grains,
his feet—banished
nests stitched in sand,
light years from resurrection.

May his ash shed
in us.

§

Pause to imagine a mynah bird from Syria
and a mynah bird from old Europe, placed in the same cage. An
experiment. All they can do is stare at each other.

§

Now, have a beautiful bird's tale of a day.

THE OCEAN HUMS FABLES
IN THE BOY'S EAR

Each stroke of my wave caresses your cheek.
I give you a manatee to dive with.

Hunting for home
was the dark business.

To the imprint of repetition.

How deep is true?

I go in the night,
catch prayers

to break the lull of the waves.

MOTHER'S PREMONITION

Tiny grebe beats his heart
against the kitchen window,

a dervish,
a child in prayer,

What stone is measured in seeds?

Last year, after you left,
a bird flew in—

What is the glass in me—
what bird is tapping there?

What offerings can I give
to wake you?

DYBBUK OF ANNUNCIATIONS

Beams of light refract in dense
liquid where I am trapped.

I move in wedges,
the water measured
in drifts of stone.

I trap too much light.

When a person dies,
people put jars with water around the house
for the soul to quench its thirst.

I died in water, immersed in a jar
of ocean, yet my soul over and over
dies of thirst until I quench inside you.

Let yourself explore my wound.

The solemn lives there.

MOTHER DREAMS OF HER SON

The mountain is a ring, a cadence.
Tree crowns, clumps of green with blue,
swelling, sound the one mystery note,
orbit their girth, our longing steady.

Between you and me a tree took root,
a bird raged its hollows,
seeds of ring scattered onto the sod.

DYBBUK ON THE WIRES OF A DREAM

Let there be a house

where Earth is air, where itineraries slide
into shards, debris, nests in windbreaks.

I have lived centuries under ice.

What was my first syllable?
What did its light obscure?

Pictographs cradle in the air. Images
decomposed into morphemes.

A SETTLER WATCHING FROM THE SHORE

A refugee washed ashore. I watch him walking on thin strips of
land between the rivulets of water, the surfaces
streaked over with grebes' feathers.
Am I to bury him with metaphors? Thorns of boats, freefalls,
footnotes. *Coterminous with longing.*
Vagrant birds never tire of reeds. His heart a capsized boat,
the boy faces the beach, bound for the island of Kos,
which means a blackbird in my language of loss.
I see a migrant pebbling the shores.
A refugee dips his pain one-hundred fold.
A fire rises. Stardust rusts.

Dybbuk Whispers

I need to be inside you
in order to live.
In me, you hear whimpering
of drowned children,
they walk in circles.

We walk in circles,
gathering all the rings and foxes, Nantucket knots.
All the words. If we were to have all the birds, all
the ferns, particles and saints;
all the yellow birch, eye-salmon rose,
fiddlehead ferns, ruffed grouse, a flock of sea-horses...

What could we offer in exchange for one child?

WHAT HAPPENS TO A CURSE?

Does it roam the woods,
circle over the roofs,
swarm in sprouts,
simmer in solitude?
Snap, as the dybbuk would,
when thrown out of the tree.
(Crystaled ferocity)

In every curse, the demise of yes,
carved into basswood bark.

THE DROWNED BOY PLAYING ON THE BEACH

Ring a ring o'roses, a pocketful of posies, a-tishoo
a-tishoo, we all fall down.
Ring bark
Ring bone
Ring of the Nibelung
Ring stone
Ring tall
Ring toss
Ring worm
A ring of sea horses
The heyday of the ring
Ring scars
Ring of baobabs
Rings on yellow-shafted flickers

Ring wrung wrong

I rise to the sound of rings.
Most of the time I cannot stand silence.

OF ANNUNCIATIONS

Limping for presence.

Tired of wrestling
with the dybbuk
who could do nothing
to unearth me.

My weary litany:
the world exists
my body does not.

In the absence of me, your world
chants me back.

I watch wild turkeys
feeding on tiny seeds
of my nouns.

THE DROWNED BOY ON AN ISLAND

White gleams. Trees inflamed in white.
The white on the trees hurts.

Torn between
obedience to gods.

Torn pieces of a wedding dress.

The boy slays a chameleon;
another epiphyte grows.

Knot topology:
the structure of string coming and going—
slanged, slung, sung.

Out of the labyrinth of bubbles,
cams, pulleys, circuits, gears,
wheels with teeth.

Words, curves,
worm gear
pushing the cam,
turning the spindle.

(every child a little atomist, a Diogenes.)

BOY'S MOTHER

Deserted for her holiness,
she dies her deaths
through water.

He writes to her on child-like paper.
She makes paper boats on which he
will ride back.

Do monsters have monsters?

Refugee Mother Ruminates

Something that is something that was,
what was and is not.
How black is black?
Can you draw out Leviathan with a fishhook,
press down his tongue with a cord?

Now, the procession of faces
to the white host,
to surrender
(even suffering was not ours).

I am cleaning the bark you brought,
the wood that grows.

I cheat reality, chasing and catching small birds.

THE BOY VISITS GUADALUPE

The earth is a quadrangle floating on a great body of water.
In the center rises a sacred mountain with a cave,
at the entrance of which grows a ceiba tree.
Who is He who holds a jaguar head?
Saints are fully in their jacarandas, in love
with purples. On the tree a peacock sits, yet another
apparition of the Madonna. Rumors on photographic plates.
Sunset, a splash of red turtle. Frogs dressed in blue,
sacrificed and roasted. Women and children kept
in their houses, for fear they'd transform into wild animals.

Triangular blossom on her tilma — both a heart with its arteries
and a flower with its pulsing color.
What demons await this sacrifice?
This Lady says that, without tearing them out,
we should place them in her hands
so that she may then present them
to the true God.

Morenita, Mother of *mestizi* —
products of conquest and rape,
Nahuatl — my dear Mother
of ruffed grouse,
on your tunic show me
the four-petaled jasmine
the indigenous knew
as *Nabui Ollin*, "always
in the movement."

Virgin of the motion,
I search for food in the animals' stalls.

Multiply four petals into eight.
Oh, planet Venus
into tulip trees.
Oh, morning star
into sphere, a ring,
a binding circumference.
Oh, birth in pregnancy
into breathing.

A TREE CARRIES THE EPIPHYTES, THE MOSQUES

A tree carries the epiphytes, the mosques
of insects, the sickle-wing guans,
the bromeliad flowers,
until it collapses.

The cross is a way
of now. Through cracks
it carries the light.

Cecropia trees are silver mosques
of maternity. A potoo bird perches
for hours on the stump of a dead tree.

The leaves turn into green-crown wood nymphs,
orange-bellied euphonias and tanagers.

Black solitaires fly away.

The Inca women
carry jugs of water and children
until the weight roots them,
until the earth is smaller.

Sacri-ficio – to make holy

The bleeding-heart flowers.
The span of luna moths' lives
lies in their 10-day intensity.
Hair grows on dead trees.

A ficus tree will drop
its seed into another tree
and grow around the host tree
until both hollow out.

§

The trees flame in white
brides-sky, icicles
thaw in the river, in the psalm
beating within our ears.

Each beat has a mystic in it,
with dazzling feet.

"Perfect tenderness in the body"—
Gift, fidelity,

and fear of gaps in the concrete.

Listen, a bird is winging back!

Its feathers, luminous
pieces of gold, smelted, malleable,

shaped in the wax of bees
burnished to reflect light.

MOTHER GUADALUPE LEANS OVER THE REFUGEE BOY'S BODY, SHE WHISPERS

you would prefer only the part of that tree
you would you would the part only
the part you would of that tree would
its crown its bronchioles yet it grows
it grows and bifurcates until the whole
it grows it grows it grows the whole
until the whole until the whole develops
develops out of its fragment
out of out of it develops fragment the whole
always emerges out of its fragment
a whole a thorny crown
a thorny crown a thorny thorny

all inward forces clash and iterate to shape a single leaf
inward clash and iterate iterate to shape inward and inward clash
single leaf clash and iterate clash and clash a single leaf yes you
would you would this single leaf this fragment
and yes you would and yes this single single without
it grows and bifurcates grows and bifurcates
grows into such thorny crown such thorny love
the Gethsemane

the owl is a clock
measuring your blood vessels an owl is a clock
each nerve falls in a split capillary second
split capillary falls split each nerve
falls an unbitten apple it falls each nerve
each dying child becomes a fractal becomes
unbitten apple unbitten falls becomes

each Syrian boy becomes becomes broken coastline
each refugee breath branches and divides
branches and branches and divides
not a milligram of flesh will be taken without spilling
blood without blood spilling you will not run
you will not run broken
a speck and the universe
of one cell both speck and universe
bigger than its surface topology this cell and cell surface
and topology both speck and speck

the line of infinite affection squeezed into limited space
both speck and universe of one cell of limited space
now it spreads infinite affection attracts
the iteration of one gaze of one of one attracts
a small gaze expanding like a shade
a small gaze a small shade limited space expands
someone is catching sunbeams

ANNUNCIATION OF DYBBUK

My burial complete, through numerous prayers
in mosques, temples, shrines, churches and pilgrimages.
I yearn to exist. I snag tails of words and eat them
to break the silence. Those offered to host me,
how will they know me? When I swim out into them,
I will do so with luminous blue levity—the thinnest, translucent
slips of vellum. I gather
flitting and darting finches.
I stare at houses that stare right through me.

WAITING FOR THE SOUL

We put an extra plate on Xmas Eve table,
in case we hear a knocking on our window-sill
(will he like *kompot* and *pierogi?*)
(will he like to play the Scrabble?).

We put little boats and birds on each
branch of the tree.

We will play hide-and-seek
inside the tree.

We will show him
the tenderness of the hedgehog
in all its bristles.

I will teach him how to call back to mirsi,
so the bird whistles back to us and takes us
to where wild honey lives in the trees.

Like the Boni tribe, we will shin up the trees
and pay the bird generously with wax
& bee larvae.

DREAMS OF FOXES

Making music with its bone, fox triangulates—
each muscle a prayer clasped in attention.
Each muscle fulfills its destiny. Caress. Arch.
An arc of *wu wei* to find that point in space. Astute dive towards
innocence. Fox eats like a saint,

making music with its bone. With seven doors,
a vole under the snow,

fox puts branches in the holes.
It bites the snake's head,
swings it against a marigold tree
into its sainthood.

BOY'S MOTHER READS HIM UNDER THE WATER

The fox had his mind made up before the flood.
We domesticated him, feeding him leaves
of the Bible. We confused psalm for a sunrise.
We went barefoot in the snow.

He avoids hunters, puts branches in the holes and when attacked
by snakes, will turn his back
and bite the snake's head, swing it
against the marigold tree.

"Fox," a word we did not catch to break.

A Migrant Beggar

He taps on our car window.
I give him 30 dollars.
Pray for us, we say.

He worked construction;
got a wound—
no insurance.

Now he calls it a day.
His is the kingdom.

I close the windows, drive off.
Augustine's *Confessions*
flutter on the back seat.

I see him again when I turn
the corner, God with an amputated leg,

He looks shattered.
His tears tap the rhythm on my windows.

OF ANNUNCIATIONS

Theresa of Avila wrote *morada*
for "walking away."

There is an immigrant in our soul.

The feet of the Syrian boy washed ashore.

In each of us, the feet of an Archangel.

Afterword on Dybbuk and Annunciation

In Jewish mysticism and folklore, a dybbuk is the displaced soul of a dead person. It is popularly believed to be a "clinging spirit"—a disturbed soul that possesses us. Such a spirit that seeks revenge or justice is juxtaposed in Jewish Kabbalah with an ibbur, a benevolent, temporary, and at times voluntary possession. While dybbuks possess, ibburs, in a sense, bless.

While the living ones can sometimes give permission for an ibbur to inhabit them or spiritually impregnate them (the meaning of the word *ibbur*), dybbuks enter living persons without permission. Without a proper burial, the soul is compelled to go astray and manifests itself as a dybbuk.

My book deliberately complicates the binary between dybbuk and ibbur. One of the questions I pose is: *"What becomes of the souls of drowned refugees who do not have a proper burial?"* While using the word dybbuk, I do not intend, however, to present them as malicious and vengeful souls. Instead, I want to redefine and rehabilitate dybbuk by merging its characteristics with ibbur (whose name I never mention in the book, to eschew the binary). Dybbuk in this book yearns to exist until its conflict is resolved and therefore it sneaks into another body in order to fulfill its mission.

Sometimes, it simply enters a body because it is lost. It fills the host's body and soul with pining, misery, or, rage and aggression depending on its intent. Needless to say, dybbuks are unpredictable and can cause havoc and torment, but can also lead to restitution. The breaking of the boundary between dybbuk and ibbur has been performed before. Just to give you more of the idea, in *Musical Variations on Jewish Thought*, Revault D'Allonnes writes:

"[W]hat is intolerable to Jewish thought is the idea that a being can die before fulfilling his destiny; the dybbuk is the spirit of one who has died 'prematurely,' and takes possession of a living person in order to try, as it were, to conclude his role, to round out his existence. It is not a ghost seeking vengeance or asserting its rights. It is a person making himself complete, fulfilling himself, wiping out the error or horror of early death. A phantom is hostile, ill-disposed, frightening. The dybbuk is good, it returns in order to do good; if the community wants to get rid of it . . . that is because it disturbs the social order. But, in doing so, it carries out the divine order. In this sense, which is the sense of truth, the dybbuk is an object of love. Love which is a scandal and disgrace to partisans of order but certainty and happiness to those on the side of justice..."

Annunciation in this book extrapolates from the religious event, described in the New Testament by Luke, in which Archangel Gabriel announces to Mary that she will become the Mother of God. Mary responds to the visitor: "Be it Done According to Thy Word." The Archangel represents the other, a stranger in whom Mary trusts. I attempt to map the biblical event onto the migration crises of this current historical moment, in which settlers and volunteers (as I call them in the book) encounter the strangers, refugees, migrants. My intention was to also symbolize the term further, as well as stretch its connotations. Annunciation becomes a symbol of the "yes" that we utter in front of reality, particularly confronted with the exiles, strangers—in other words, the other.

On another level, there are also Archangels in the book that appear to the migrants, encouraging them to flee the danger.

95

The book meditates on these various "yeses". It quivers on the brink between openness to the other and the terror the other brings out in us. *What does it mean to say "yes" to a stranger? What implications, threats, blessings and responsibilities do "yes" carry? Can we say "yes" to a dislocated soul in order to become more fully who we were meant to be?*

NOTES

from Mark 8:24

From the documentary film: Io Sto Con La Sposa

Title - adaptation of Psalm 33:7
San Miniato – Christian hermit and martyr of Armenian descent
who lived in Florence, Italy. He was persecuted and beheaded by
the Emperor Decius (249-251 A.D.). Allegedly, after beheading, he
picked up his head, crossed the Arno and walked up the hill of Mons
Fiorentinus to his hermitage, where he died. The shrine first, and
then the basilica San Miniato, were erected there in his name.

A quote from Mirabai's poem "Mira The Lotus" in Mirabai: Ecstatic
Poems. Versions by Robert Bly, Jane Hirshfield, Beacon Press, 2004,
p. 63.

Psalm 46:10

Inspired by the photography exhibit, Exilium by Marta
Bogdańska, Warsaw, Poland July 2016. All the characters are real and
their objects factual.

Various translations & appropriations of Exodus 22:21.

Acknowledgments

I am grateful and honored that Omnidawn Publishing has provided a home for my poems. This is my second book with them and I am very happy to be embraced by such a fantastic publishing team.

Grateful acknowledgment is made to Sam Witt, the editor of *Devouring the Green: fear of a human planet, an Anthology of New Writing*, which published seven poems from *Of Annunciations*. A few poems from the book were translated into Italian and published in *La freccia e il cerchio*. Thanks to the Italian translator, Mariadonata Villa, as well as the editors.

Other poems from the book appeared or are forthcoming in *Solstice* and *Spoon River Poetry*.

I am grateful to Marta Ceroni, who featured some of the poems at the 2016 Annual Meeting of The Balaton Group in Budapest, Hungary.

Humble appreciation to Meghan Udell whose personal narrative of volunteering at a refugee camp in Lesbos, Greece inspired verse that made its way into the book.

Thanks to Marta Bogdańska, a Polish photographer, whose 2016 exhibit *Exilium*, in Warsaw, Poland inspired the poem of the same name.

My gratitude goes to Julie Püttgen who designed the cover for this and my previous Omnidawn book, *Contraband of Hoopoe*.

Thanks as well to Teresa Cader, and Zachary Finch for their invaluable support and suggested revisions. Thanks to Agnieszka Ginko-Humphries, a Polish poet, who gave me encouragement and faith in the book's importance. Thanks to Toney Brinkley and Craig Greenman, who read a very early draft and provided me with comments. Thanks to Tom Kealy for the initial inspiration for this book.

And thanks to Ruth White & George Greene whose house full of birds witnessed the origin of *Of Annunciations* and most of its revision.

Special thanks to my husband, Eric DeLuca, who reviewed the manuscript within the editing process.

photo by: Michael Seamans

Ewa Chrusciel is a bilingual poet and a translator. Her two previous books in English are *Contraband of Hoopoe* (Omnidawn Press, 2014) and *Strata* (Emergency Press, 2011) and she also published three books in Polish: *Furkot* (2001), *Sopiłki* (2009), and *Tobołek* (2016). Her poems appeared in numerous journals and anthologies in USA, Italy, and Poland. Her translations of American and Polish poets appeared in numerous anthologies and journals in USA and Poland, as well as in a book. She also translated into Polish: "White Fang" by Jack London, "The Shadow Line" by Joseph Conrad, and "More Stories from My Father's Court" by Isaac Bashevis Singer. She is an Associate Professor of Humanities (Creative Writing) at Colby-Sawyer College in New Hampshire, USA.

Of Annunciations
by Ewa Chrusciel

Cover painting by Julie Püttgen:
Cloudmapping: Next Gate, 2008.
Watercolor and gouache on paper, 16 x 12 inches
www.108namesofnow.com & www.unlessanduntil.info.

Cover typeface: Trajan Pro & Garamond 3 LT Std
Interior typefaces: Garamond 3 LT Std, Trajan Pro,
& Palatino LT Std

Cover & Interior design by Cassandra Smith

Offset printed in the United States
by Edwards Brothers Malloy, Ann Arbor, Michigan
On 55# Enviro Natural 100% Recycled 100% PCW
Acid Free Archival Quality FSC Certified Paper

Publication of this book was made possible in part by gifts from:
The Clorox Company
The New Place Fund
Robin & Curt Caton

Omnidawn Publishing
Oakland, California
2017
Rusty Morrison & Ken Keegan, senior editors & co-publishers
Gillian Olivia Blythe Hamel, managing editor
Cassandra Smith, poetry editor & book designer
Sharon Zetter, poetry editor, book designer & development officer
Avren Keating, poetry editor, fiction editor & marketing assistant
Liza Flum, poetry editor
Juliana Paslay, fiction editor
Gail Aronson, fiction editor
Trisha Peck, marketing assistant
Cameron Stuart, marketing assistant
Natalia Cinco, marketing assistant
Maria Kosiyanenko, marketing assistant
Emma Thomason, administrative assistant
SD Sumner, copyeditor
Kevin Peters, *OmniVerse* Lit Scene editor
Sara Burant, *OmniVerse* reviews editor